Recognizing and Adapting to Unrestricted Warfare Practices by China

Bryan K. Luke

AIR WAR COLLEGE

AIR UNIVERSITY

RECOGNIZING AND ADAPTING TO UNRESTRICTED WARFARE PRACTICES BY CHINA

by

Bryan K. Luke, COL, USA

A Research Report Submitted to the Faculty

In Partial Fulfillment of the Graduation Requirements

15 February 2012

DISCLAIMER

Biography

Colonel Bryan Luke is a U.S. Army Infantry officer assigned to the Air War College, Air University, Maxwell AFB, AL. He graduated from Auburn University in 1988 with a Bachelor of Arts degree in Business Management, the Colorado School of Mines in 1998 with a Master's of Science in Mineral Economics and the U.S. Army's School of Advanced Military Studies in 2002 with a Masters of Military Arts and Science. He has served in leadership positions in both light and mechanized infantry units from platoon to brigade levels. He has also served on the Army Staff and Joint Staff where he was involved with force development planning and analysis and joint concept development and experimentation.

Abstract

In 1999, two Chinese Colonels published a concept paper which advocated that China adopt an "Unrestricted Warfare" (URW) strategy to respond to U.S. power and military superiority. Over the last 10 years, the Chinese government seems to have implemented elements of this strategy to erode U.S. world power and influence. Due to its cultural, doctrinal, and legal biases and constraints, the United States has experienced difficulty in recognizing and responding effectively to URW practices. If the U.S. hopes to deter, prevent, and/or respond to all forms of current and future URW threats, it must make policy and organizational changes within its government and the military.

A primary reason why the U.S. is experiencing difficulty in adapting to URW practices is the difference in the thoughts and approach to warfare by the U.S. and the Chinese. The American way of conducting warfare has been greatly influenced by European authors and militaries that advocate that warfare as a physically violent action to compel an enemy to bend to your will and agree to your terms. Therefore, America fights wars of attrition and annihilation against its opponents and is best prepared for combat against symmetrical, regular enemy forces rather than asymmetrical ones. As with America and the West, the Chinese way of war is greatly influenced by its history and culture. The teachings of Confucius and Sun Zi, are of particular significance. These men taught obedience to the state, the primacy of relationships over law, and the importance of deception and surprise in warfare and the affairs of state. As a result, Chinese military and civilian leaders often prefer an indirect approach in warfare and in its dealings with other nations.

Since the publication of the URW concept paper, Chinese leaders seem to have adapted and implemented many of the author's ideas in its dealings with the U.S. Although the concept contains 26 forms of URW (which include both military and non-military forms), the non-military forms of URW are the ones the U.S. has experienced most difficulty. My paper highlights examples of Chinese URW practices in the areas of Lawfare, Economic Warfare, and Cyber-Warfare.

Although the U.S. has made improvements to identify and respond to some key URW challenges over the last 10 years, our current approach continues to be heavily military focused. To adequately deter, prevent, and/or respond to URW attacks in the future, the U.S. must first consider expanding the definition of what actions are considered an "act of war" to include actions/activities beyond actual kinetic attacks. Second, intelligence assets/organizations should be organized and trained to identify economic and financial threats and attacks. And finally, the current U.S. strategy for network/cyber-warfare is too defensively focused to be an effective deterrence against cyber-attacks. To be effective at deterrence, the strategy must include both an effective denial and punishment capability.

Introduction

What does it mean when a nation decides to go to war? Clausewitz's defines it as the "*use of force* to compel another to do our will" and as "a clash between major interest, which is *resolved by bloodshed*."[1] Since the collapse of the Soviet Union and the end of the Cold War, we have seen a rise in warfare practices by both nation states and non-state actors that seemingly follow no rules and often use tools/methods other than force to accomplish their objectives. This type of warfare has often been referred to as being asymmetric, unconventional, or unrestricted. In 1999 two Chinese Colonels, Qiao Liang and Wang Xiangsui, published a paper advocating that China adopt an "Unrestricted Warfare" (URW) strategy to respond to U.S. power and military superiority.[2] Over the last 10 years, the Chinese government seems to have implemented elements of this strategy to erode U.S. world power and influence in an attempt to decrease our national will and ability to prevent the Chinese from accomplishing regional goals/objectives and obtaining peer status.

Given its liberal democratic values with its cultural, doctrinal, and legal biases and constraints, the United States has experienced great difficulty in recognizing and responding effectively to URW practices. Even so, since 9-11, the U.S. has made some changes to how its government and military are organized, trained, and equipped to respond to URW challenges. Unfortunately, these changes are not enough and further policy and organization measures are needed if the U.S. hopes to deter, prevent, and/or respond to all forms of current and future URW threats.

What is Unrestricted Warfare?

In their 1999 concept paper, Chinese Colonels Qiao Liang and Wang Xiangsui described URW as "using all means whatsoever… means that involve military power and means that do not involve military power, means that entail casualties and means that do not entail casualties…to force the enemy to serve one's own interests. In short, warfare that transcends all boundaries and limits can be considered unrestricted warfare."[3] Colonel Liang and Xiangsui identified 26 forms of URW which are summarized in the Table 1 (definitions in appendix A).

Table 1: Forms of Unrestricted Warfare[4]

Military	Trans-Military	Non-Military
Atomic Warfare	Diplomatic Warfare	Financial Warfare
Conventional Warfare	Network Warfare	Trade Warfare
Bio-Chemical Warfare	Intelligence Warfare	Resources Warfare
Space Warfare	Psychological Warfare	Economic Aid Warfare
Electronic Warfare	Smuggling Warfare	Sanctions Warfare
Guerrilla Warfare	Drug Warfare	Regulations Warfare
Terrorist Warfare	Fabrication Warfare	Ecological Warfare
	Tactical Warfare	Ideological Warfare
	Technological Warfare	Media Warfare
		Cultural Warfare

They further expand on this concept by advocating that:

> "While we are seeing a relative reduction in military violence, at the same time we are seeing an increase in political, economic, and technological violence…If we acknowledge that the new principles of war are no longer using armed forces to compel the enemy to submit to one's will, but rather are using all means, including armed force or non-armed force, military and non-military, and lethal and non-lethal means to compel the enemy to accept one's interest, then this represents a change in war (from the accepted definition of war) and a change in the mode of war."[5]

The U.S. currently does not have an agreed upon definition for Unrestricted Warfare. Instead, U.S. doctrine and military writings express the ideas of URW primarily across two different concepts; irregular warfare and hybrid warfare. Joint Publication 1-02 defines irregular warfare (IW) as "a violent struggle among state and non-state actors for legitimacy and influence over the relevant population(s). IW favors indirect and asymmetric approaches, though it may employ the full range of military and other capacities, in order to erode an adversary's power, influence, and will."[6]

The Counsel for Emerging National Security Affairs recently published a book containing multiple essays on unconventional approaches to warfare titled *Hybrid Warfare and Transnational Threats*.[7] In this book, author Frank Hoffman quotes Secretary of Defense Robert Gates as stating "we can expect to see more tools and tactics of destruction, from the sophisticated to the simple, being employed simultaneously in hybrid and more complex forms of warfare…the categories of warfare are blurring and do not fit into neat, tidy boxes."[8] Mr Hoffman terms this complex and simultaneous blurring of various modes of conflict as hybrid warfare. He further defines a hybrid threat as "any state or non-state adversary that simultaneously and adaptively employs a fused mix of conventional weapons, irregular tactics, terrorism, and criminal behavior to obtain their political objectives."[9]

What the U.S. concepts have in common with the Chines definition of URW is an approach to war that utilizes both military and non-military means to achieve desired objectives. Therefore, for the purposes of this paper, I define Unrestricted Warfare as *the employment of the full range of military and non-military means, both lethal and non-lethal, to obtain desired political objectives and/or erode an adversary's power, influence, and will.*

Differences in Western and Chinese Thought and Approach

The American Way of War

The American way of conducting warfare has been greatly influenced by the writings of such renowned authors as Carl Von Clausewitz and Baron Antoine Jomini. Whereas Clausewitz provided a theoretical strategic framework for warfare where "war is a continuation of policy by other means," Jomini provided the basis for much of the America's operational level doctrine for "how to" conduct wars.[10] Both of these men saw warfare as a physically violent action to compel an enemy to bend to your will and agree to your terms.[11] In his 1973 book, *The American Way of War: A History of United States Military Strategy and Policy*, author Russell F. Weigley supports this view of American warfare by stating that America fights wars of attrition and annihilation against its opponents.[12] British Strategist Colin Gray believes that there are 13 key characteristics in the American way of war.[13] Gray's characteristics show the U.S. as a country best prepared for combat against a symmetrical, regular enemy rather than an asymmetrical one.[14] Gray argues that one of the main reasons America has problems with Irregular Warfare (IW) is that it is not just a military effort; it must be a whole of government endeavor if it is to have any hope for success. Integrating and synchronizing a whole of government approach into a war has often proven difficult, if not impossible for America unless there is a clear threat or challenge to a critical national interest. Another reason for this integration difficulty is due to what author Rose Keravuori defines as the American way of war; two distinct methodologies which consist of a "tactical way of battle and a strategic way of war."[15] The tactical way of battle involves a style of warfare where distinct American attributes define the use of force (i.e. Colin Gray's characteristics), while the strategic way of war is attuned to the whims of a four year political system which creates difficulties in turning tactical victories into strategic success as well as difficulties in integrating the whole-of-government into the endeavor.

Another significant influence on the American way of war is "just war theory." JWT has "three fundamental aims: to explain when armed force may be used; to limit the resort to force whenever possible; and to contain the damage done in and by warfare."[16] The impact of JWT has been to formalize a set of rules and limits on warfare. The codification of these rules began in the mid-nineteenth century during the American Civil War and accelerated after WWII. The most well-known of these set of rules is the Geneva Convention. As of 2009, every member state of the United Nations (UN) was a party to the four Geneva Conventions.

The Chinese Way of War

As with America and the West, the Chinese way of war is greatly influenced by its history and culture. The teachings of Confucius and Sun Zi, are of particular significance. Confucianism dominated Chinese society for over 2,000 years. Confucianism is primarily a humanitarian focused set of beliefs and values that stresses the importance of family (filial Piety), ritual, loyalty, meritocracy, relationships, and the desire to avoid shame and losing face.[17] Chinese rulers often used Confucianism as a kind of "state religion" where its authoritarianism, paternalism and submission to authority aspects were used as political tools to keep the population in line.[18] Additionally, Chinese leaders were often reluctant to employ well defined laws because relationships were considered more important than the laws themselves. As a result, China was dominated by a government of nepotism, favoritism, and an ill-defined legal system for almost 2000 years. With its primary focus on keeping the internal systems of China in harmony, the military strategy of the Confucian ruler was often defensive in nature, with a goal of maintaining ones borders and keeping potential enemies weak and divided.

The Ancient Chinese military general, philosopher, and strategists Sun Zi is well known for his essay/book, *The Art of War*. As one of only a handful of military texts to have survived before the unification of China in the 2nd Century BC, *The Art of War* was a central part of the *Seven Military Classics* which formed the foundation of orthodox military theory in China.[19] The *Art of War* was required reading to pass the tests needed for imperial appointments to key military positions.[20] A key philosophy of Sun Zi was that "being victorious a hundred times in a hundred battles is not the most excellent approach. Causing the enemy forces to submit without a battle is the most excellent approach."[21] For Sun Zi, war was more of a psychological contest, with the use of force having a limited role.[22] A key point from Sun Zi about deception was that "it is not just about denying information to an enemy; it is meant primarily to induce him to act in ways that are beneficial to oneself."[23] The following quote from Sun Zi's establishes this fact clearly.

> "All warfare is based on deception. Therefore, when capable, feign incapacity; when active, inactivity. When near, make it appear that you are far away; when far away, that you are near. Offer the enemy a bait to lure him; feign disorder and strike him. Anger his general and confuse him. Pretend inferiority and encourage his arrogance. Attack where he is unprepared; sally out when he does not expect you. These are the strategist's keys to victory."[24]

China's current way of war incorporates many of the philosophies of both Confucius and Sun Zi. In the early 1990's China's leader, Deng Xiaoping, gave guidance to China's foreign policy and military personnel that China should: "observe calmly; secure our position, cope with affairs calmly; hide our capacities and bide our time; be good at maintaining a low profile, and never claim leadership.[25] This "24 Character" strategy "suggests both a short-term desire to downplay China's capabilities and avoid confrontation, and a long-term strategy to build up China's power to maximize options for the future."[26]

In 2003, China's leaders began promoting their "peaceful rise strategy" in response to those who claimed that conflict between a rising power and the current powers was inevitable. This concept was re-affirmed by Chinese authorities in a 2011 in a white paper on China's national policy goals.[27] The paper's key message was that "China's peaceful development has broken away from the traditional pattern where a rising power was bound to seek hegemony… the central goal of China's diplomacy is to create a peaceful and stable international environment for its development." To support this policy, China's official military strategy is stated to be "purely defensive in nature" with a focus on "active-defense," enhancing its "national strategic capabilities" and maintaining China's "no first use policy on nuclear weapons."[28]

Although this strategy appears to enjoy widespread acceptance among Beijing's foreign and security policy establishment, detailed study of Chinese military and academic writings reveal differences of opinion concerning the *means* of achieving China's broad national objectives.[29] Chinese military strategists characterize active-defense as "adhering to the principle feature of defensive operations, self-defense and striking and getting the better of the enemy only after the enemy has started an attack."[30] However, an analysis of their writings leaves in doubt as to the threshold for "an enemy first starting an attack." The 2011 Report to Congress on the "Military and Security Developments Involving the People's Republic of China" highlights the fact that the Chinese military definition of an enemy strike is not limited to conventional, kinetic operations. An enemy "strike" may also be defined in political terms whereby political actions can be interpreted as "acts of war" which warrant a military and/or non-military response in the name of defense."[31]

This idea of pre-emptive actions conducted prior to armed conflict fits well with the Chinese history and culture of warfare with its focus on surprise, deception, and the indirect approach. The fact that Colonel's Liang and Xiangsui's Unrestricted Warfare (URW) concept was read by then Chinese President Jiang Zemin and Defense Minister Chi Haotian provides an indication on the importance that the Chinese place on such ideas. The PLA Academy of Military Science also advocates that "war is not only a military struggle, but also a comprehensive contest on fronts of politics, economy, diplomacy, and law."[32] In 2003 the Chinese Communist Party (CCP) Central Committee endorsed the concept of "Three Warfares." Borrowing from the ideas in the URW paper, this concept specifically advocated the use of psychological warfare, media warfare, and legal warfare (lawfare) to undermine the spirit and ideological commitment of an adversary before and during a conflict, weaken international support for the opponent's cause, and reinforce China's domestic support for military operations.[33]

"Friendly Competition" or Unrestricted Warfare Strategy?

Are Chinese actions/activities over the last 10 years since the release of Colonel's Liang and Xiangsui's Unrestricted Warfare concept a calculated strategy utilizing URW techniques to erode U.S. power and influence in the Asia-Pacific region while enhancing China's? Or, are they simply standard competitive practices among great powers? I do not have a definitive answer to these questions, but given China's history, culture, and military and political strategy discussed so far, it is more likely than not that China's actions are a calculated effort vice simple competition. Over the next several paragraphs, I will discuss potential examples of Chinese URW practices in the areas of Lawfare, Economic Warfare, and Network Warfare and let the reader decide if these actions are just "friendly competition."

Lawfare

Lawfare, also known as legal or regulations warfare, is simply "the use of law as a means to obtain military or political objectives."[34] The intent of lawfare is to use the tools of domestic and international law to "legitimize" one's claims in the eyes of the international community and to manage any possible political repercussions in the event of military action. Lawfare can also be employed to hamstring an adversary's operational freedom and shape the operational space.[35] Harvard Law Professor David Kennedy states that "law today can often accomplish what we might once have done with bombs and missiles: seize and secure territory, send messages about resolve and political seriousness, and even break the will of a political opponent"[36]

China has attempted to employ legal warfare in the maritime domain and in international airspace in pursuit of an increased security buffer zone and to gain control of additional natural resources. The United Nations Convention on the Law of the Sea (UNCLOS), which China is a signatory, allows any country the sovereign right to conduct economic or resource management activities in an exclusive economic zone (EEZ) up to 200 nautical miles from its shores. In the 1930s, China began publishing regional maps which showed the *entire* South China Sea as part of its territory. After taking power in 1949, the Chinese Communist Party continued to maintain this claim.[37] China also interprets the UNCLOS as meaning that no surveillance or military activity or any kind can be conducted by foreign nations within the exclusion zone. Since 2005, Chinese Navy assets and civilian enforcement ships have increasingly harassed, seized, or threatened foreign military vessels, civilian fishing boats, research ships, and drilling and exploration vessels throughout the South China and Yellow Seas (often far beyond the 200 mile EEZ). With its efforts, China is "attempting to shape international opinion in favor of a distorted interpretation of the UN Convention on the Law of the Sea by moving scholarly opinion and national perspectives away from long-accepted norms of freedom of navigation and toward interpretations of increased sovereign authority over the 200 nautical mile Exclusive Economic Zone, the airspace above it, and possibly outer space."[38]

China, knowing that our society respects the rule of law and that it demands compliance with it, has also consistently attempted to block U.S. actions to employ diplomatic, economic, or military actions against rouge nations through the use of its veto power in the United Nations Security Council. The Chinese are well aware that "in modern popular democracies, even a limited armed conflict requires a substantial base of public support and that support can erode or even reverse itself rapidly if people believe that the war is being conducted in an unfair, inhumane, or iniquitous way."[39] Many of our closest allies have often been reluctant to enact sanctions or take part in military operations against other nations unless the UN has endorsed such action. As a result of China's effective use of lawfare, humanitarian abuses and criminal actions by rogue regimes continue to occur throughout the world and the U.S. is often forced to take unilateral and ineffective measures against these countries.

Economic Warfare

Encyclopedia Britannica defines economic warfare as:

> "The use or threat of use, of economic means against a country in order to weaken its economy and thereby reduce its political and military power.... It also includes the use of economic means to compel an adversary to change its policies or behavior or to undermine its ability to conduct normal relations with other countries."[40]

Although "economic warfare" is not a term identified by Colonel's Liang and Xiangsui, its definition encompasses five of their URW categories: financial warfare, trade warfare, resources warfare, economic aid warfare, and sanctions warfare.

China now has the second-largest economy in the world and has frequently been described as likely to surpass both Europe and the U.S. in total GDP by 2020. Trade, investment, and foreign aid/assistance are behind much of the PRC's recent inroads throughout the developing world.[41] In Latin America, Africa, and the Middle East, Chinese companies, in coordination with the Chinese government and banks, have begun to make multibillion dollar loans and investments, creating a rapidly expanding presence of Chinese companies and workers in the region in such sectors as construction, logistics, manufacturing, telecommunications, and retail.[42] Chinese foreign assistance and investment is especially attractive to many developing countries because it generally does not require changes in the policies or performance of recipient countries' governments.[43]

The U.S. continues to have concerns about China's currency valuation policy, its unfair trade subsidies, and lack of intellectual property rights. In his January 2009 confirmation hearing, Treasury Secretary-designee Timothy Geithner said that China was intentionally "manipulating its currency" to keep its value relative to the dollar and other currencies low so that exports were cheaper than normal market prices would dictate.[44] China also subsidizes several of its exports, such as paper products, textiles, steel, and plastics, which have resulted in the loss of significant numbers of jobs in the U.S. These practices have directly contributed to the Chinese economy's ability to grow at a rate around 10 % per year over the last 10 years.

On numerous occasions, China has threatened the U.S. with punitive economic measures. In 2010, China led a push to replace the dollar as the world's reserve currency, which would have led to drastic increases in inflation in the U.S. In early 2011, China and Russia agreed to stop trading barrels of oil based on the value of the dollar and China recently announced it will trade Iranian oil for Chinese goods instead of U.S. dollars.[45] Currently, China holds about $1.2

trillion in U.S. bills, notes and bonds. After the recent announcement of additional F-16 sales to Taiwan, senior officials at the Chinese Academy of Military Science called on the government to sell-off U.S. Treasury notes. One of their Generals publicly advocated that China could "attack the U.S. by oblique means and stealthy feints" in relation for the arms sale and "should not restrict our retaliation to merely military matters; we should adopt a strategic package of counterpunches covering politics, military affairs, diplomacy and economics to treat both the symptoms and root cause of this disease.[46]"

Network Warfare

Network, or Cyber Warfare in American terminology, is a means of dominating or subverting transnational information systems. It is described by Colonel's Liang and Xiangsui as "venturing out in secret and concealing one's identity in a type of warfare that is virtually impossible to guard against."[47] In 2002, the Chinese codified the idea of network warfare into a concept they called "Integrated Network Electronic Warfare. This concept combined the elements of electronic warfare, computer network attack, computer network defense, and computer network exploitation into one overarching concept.[48]

Since the accidental U.S. attack on the Chinese embassy in 1999, the Chinese have been increasingly suspected of launching network attacks and intrusions into U.S. military, government, education, and civilian business sector systems (see Annex C for chart of significant events from 1999-2007). In 2007 and 2008, two NASA satellites were taken control of for at least 11 minutes by hackers originating from China. In 2011, it was reported that an "unprecedented" series of cyber-attacks had taken place over the last five years against governments and corporations, to include the United Nations. The Vice President for McAfee's threat research stated that "This series of attacks is the biggest transfer of wealth in terms of intellectual property in history."[49] The type of information targeted for exfiltration often had no inherent monetary value to cybercriminals, like credit card numbers or bank account information. The US information targeted to date "could potentially benefit a nation-state defense industry, space program, selected civilian high technology industries, foreign policymakers, and foreign military planners building an intelligence picture of US defense networks, logistics, and related military capabilities that could be exploited during a crisis."[50] The analysis of the attacks by McAfee points to China as the point of origin of the attacks.

How can the U.S. be better prepared for Unrestricted Warfare Practices?

Although the U.S. has made improvements to identify and respond to some key URW challenges over the last 10 years, our current approach continues to be heavily military focused. This is likely due to the fact that the U.S. currently dominates the many of the "military" forms of URW. The "trans-military" and "non-military" realms are where the U.S. currently faces the most difficultly identifying and addressing challenges. If we are to have any hope of adequately responding to both state and non-state URW attacks in these areas in the future, additional policy and organizational changes are needed. I will discuss four recommendations in the following paragraphs.

First, in order for the U.S. to develop an effective strategy to deter, prevent, and/or respond to URW attacks, the definition of what we consider an "act of war" must be expanded to include actions/activities beyond actual kinetic attacks. The U.S. has made some recent gains in this area by declaring that some forms of network warfare can be considered an act of war. The idea of "equivalence" is that if a cyber-attack produces death, damage, destruction, or high-level disruption that a traditional military attack would cause, then the "use-of-force" can be considered as a viable option in retaliation.[51] Unfortunately, equivalence is still based on the "physical damage" a trans-military URW practice creates. It does nothing to effectively address attacks from the non-military realm of URW practices. If economic warfare was directed against the U.S., and as a result we lose a significant portion of our military capabilities, lose millions of jobs, are denied access to critical resources, and suffer an economic depression that leads to increases in crime, deaths, and in political instability in the U.S. and across the world, this is still considered just "friendly competition."

Second, intelligence assets/organizations must be organized and trained to identify economic and financial attacks/threats (i.e. trans-military and non-military) against the U.S and our allies and we must have the mechanisms in place to rapidly deny or respond to these attacks. The 2010 National Security Strategy (NSS) and National Military Strategy (NMS) acknowledge the importance of the economy to national interests and defense.[52] Unfortunately, it mostly addresses actions to "internally" improve our economic situation. Fortunately, Congress has been proactive in attempting to identify some of the "external" threats in the non-military sector. The 2011 US-China Economic and Security Review Commission Annual Report to Congress highlight the following about China:

> "For the last ten years the Commission has documented Chinese export subsidies; weapons proliferation; cyber-attacks; noncompliance with World Trade Organization obligations; forced technology transfers; military modernization; resource acquisition strategies; expansion of Chinese foreign policy interests; the Chinese military threat to Taiwan; espionage; and information control, among other issues. While China has taken some steps to engage the international community, by and large China has continued to steer policy in its own narrow self-interest at home and abroad, often without regard for international rules and norms."[53]

Although this report is a step in the right direction, it still falls short of having a dedicated system, organization, or personnel to continuously monitor and/or respond to these threats. If a trans-military or non-military attack should occur a month after this report is released, who then is responsible for identifying and responding to it?

Third, the current US strategy for network warfare is too defensively focused to be an effective deterrence against cyber-attacks. To be effective at deterrence, the strategy must include both a denial and punishment capability. You must create a posture that reduces the "intent" or desire of a threat to attack. Current cyber deterrence policy relies on the U.S. maintaining "resilient" systems that can withstand an attack or be rapidly restored or bypassed with minimal disruption. U.S. policy must change to allow pre-emptive action against the networks and countries where attacks have originated and/or *are anticipated* to originate if the source of the attack/likely attack can be determined and an intent to do us harm has been established. We must clearly identify the conditions when an actual or anticipated network attack is an act of aggression/war and then be prepared to use offensive cyber warfare and other DIME efforts to defeat, neutralize, or destroy this threat. Fortunately, new doctrine under review by the Joint Staff designed to define conditions in which the military can go on the offensive against cyber threats and what specific actions it can take, should address some of these issues.[54] Unfortunately, until the U.S. actually conducts an actual cyber-attack in response to an attack on our systems, and publically acknowledges this event, deterrence is likely to fail.

Fourth, the integration and coordination among the "whole of government" must be improved if the U.S. is to rapidly and effectively respond to URW challenges. The URW practices of the 21st Century crosses the entire DIME, as well as many aspects of the civilian economic sector. The 2010 National Security Strategy has it right by advocating "strengthening national capacity thru the whole of government approach." Unfortunately, this approach has yet to be fully embraced by the government and military bureaucracy. As the Honorable James R. Locher, who is the Executive Director of a Project on National Security Reform, stated during the 2009 Johns Hopkins URW Symposium:

> "... our organizational dysfunction undermines our ability to perform in these other (non-military) specific mission areas. We are crippled in many respects in terms of our performance because: we do not have the ability to collaborate across the government, so we cannot produce a unified effort; we, in many respects, do not plan...we clearly do not practice integrated planning across the government, so we do not have unity of purpose; we have inadequate training for our people to perform these complex missions, and almost everything is done on an ad hoc basis, whether within organizations or processes."[55]

What may be needed to address these issues is a new National Security Act or a "Goldwaters-Nichols" type act for the Interagency. This act should establish a strong, unified leadership at the federal level, empower operational leaders in the field, strengthen the strategy development and planning process, and result in the creation of a more joint cadre of security professionalism.[56] Adoption of the recommendations in The Center for Strategic and International Studies "Beyond Goldwater-Nichols" project for organizing the U.S. defense and national security apparatus to meet 21st century challenges would also address many of the concerns in this area.[57] This study addressed ways to improve national security policymaking and execution on an interagency basis as well as within the Department of Defense. Its interagency recommendations share a broad theme: they aim to get the many disparate parts of the U.S. national security structure to work together, in both planning and execution.

Conclusion

Chinese history, culture, and military doctrine/strategy make it very likely they will increase the use of URW strategies and tactics against the US to accomplish their national objectives. US history and culture biases the U.S. toward a more regular/conventional approach to warfare with the military in the lead. This bias has limited our recognition and response to URW attacks from the Chinese and others. The "Cold War" with the Soviet Union lasted for almost 50 years and involved both military and non-military means for determining which nation would be the dominant influence in the world. Comparing global influence, one commentator writes that "the Chinese threat or challenge is not likely to appear as another Soviet Union, straining to keep pace with America's military, but more likely to be an "asymmetrical superpower," one that manipulates a situation so effectively that the outcome favors Chinese interest."[58] Because of our biases toward the meaning of "war," we may not recognize that we are in another "cold" one. We must adapt our national policies, strategy, organizations, and doctrine to better recognize and defeat URW threats before we wake up one morning and realize we are the "boiling frog."

Bibliography

Boot, Max. "China's Stealth War on the U.S." *Los Angeles Times*, 20 July 2005. http://articles.latimes.com/2005/jul/20/opinion/oe-boot20

Breen, Michael, and Joshua A. Geltzer. "Asymmetric Strategies as Strategies of the Strong." *Parameters* (Spring 2011): pp. 41-55.

Bunker, Dr. Robert J. *Testimony before the U.S.-China Economic and Security Review Commission: Beijing, Unrestricted Warfare and Threat Potentials.* 29 March 2007.

Clarke, Richard A., and Robert K. Knake. *Cyber War: The Next Threat to National Security and What to Do About It.* New York, NY: Harper Collins Publishers, 2010.

Congressional Research Report on Comparing Global Influence. *China's and U.S. Diplomacy, Foreign Aid, Trade, and Investment in the Developing World.* RL34620, 15 August 2008. www.fas.org/sgp/crs/row/RL34620

Cooper, Cortez A. *Joint Anti-Access Operations: China's System-of-Systems Approach: RAND Corporation Testimony presented before the U.S. China Economic and Security Review Commission*, 27 January, 2010.

Corn, Tony. "Peaceful Rise through Unrestricted Warfare: Grand Strategy with Chinese Characteristics." *Small Wars Journal*, 5 June, 2010.

Coulter, Eric. "Analysis Support for the Interagency." Ronald R. Luman, ed., *Unrestricted Warfare Symposium, Proceedings on Combating the Unrestricted Warfare Threat: Terrorism, Resources, Economics, and Cyberspace*, The John Hopkins University Applied Physics Laboratory, March 2009. www.jhuapl.edu/urw_symposium/Proceedings/2009/Book/2009URWBook.pdf

Dale, Catherine, Nina Serafino, and Pat Towell. *Organizing the U.S. Government for National Security: Overview of the Interagency Reform Debates.* Washington DC: Congressional Research Service, Library of Congress, 2008. (CRS report for Congress, RL34505).

David, Conrad, CAPT USN. *Legal Warfare in the Near Seas: How China's Maritime Claims Impact Regional Security.* Naval War College, Newport, R.I., 2010.

Dilegge, Dave. "Are We Ready for Hybrid Wars? – Revisited," *Small Wars Journal*, 24 August 2008. http://smallwarsjournal.com/blog/2008/08/are-we-ready-for-hybrid-war-r/

Dobbins, James. "Conflict with China: Prospects, Consequences, and Strategies for Deterrence." *Rand Arroyo Center Occasional Paper*, Santa Monica, CA: Rand Corporation, 2011.

Dunlap, Charles J. Jr. "Lawfare: A Decisive Element of 21st-Century Conflicts?" *Joint Force Quarterly*, Issue 54, 3d quarter, 2009.

Echevarria II, Antulio J. "Toward an American Way of War." US Army War College, Strategic Studies Institute, Carlise, PA: 2004.

Elliott, Elison. "Economic Warfare: China Threatens U.S. Debt as WMD." *Foreign Policy Association*, 22 February, 2010. http://foreignpolicyblogs.com/2010/02/22/economic-warfare-china-threatens-debt-as-wmd/

Ellis, R. Evan. "China-Latin America Military Engagement: Good Will, Good Business, and Strategic Position." Strategic Studies Institute Monograph, U.S. Army War College, August 2011.

Friedberg, Aaron, "The Future of U.S.-China Relations: Is Conflict Inevitable?" *International Security*, Vol. 30, No. 2, Fall 2005. http://belfercenter.ksg.harvard.edu/files/is3002_pp007-045_friedberg.pdf

Gertz, Bill, "Chinese see U.S. debt as weapon in Taiwan dispute," *The Washington Times*, 10 February, 2010. http://www.washingtontimes.com/news/2010/feb/10/chinese-see-us-debt-as-weapon/?page=all

Gray, Collin. "Irregular Enemies And The Essence Of Strategy: Can The American Way Of War Adapt?" Strategic Studies Institute, U.S. Army War College, March 2006.

Harris, Shane, "China's Cyber-Militia." *National Journal*, 31 January, 2011. http://www.nationaljournal.com/magazine/china-s-cyber-militia-20080531

Harris, Shane. "China's Cyber-Militia." *National Journal Magazine*, 31 May 2008. http://www.nationaljournal.com/njmagazine/cs_20080531_6948.php

Hoffman, Frank. "Conflict in the 21st Century: The Rise of Hybrid Wars." Potomac Institute for Policy Studies, Arlington VA. December 2007.

House of Representatives. *A New U.S. Grand Strategy: Hearing before the Oversight and Investigations Subcommittee of the Committee on Armed Services.* 110th Cong., 2nd sess., 31 July, 2008.

Howard, Michael, George J. Andreopoulous, and Mark R. Shulman. *The Laws of War: Constraints on Warfare in the Western World.* Binghamton, NY: Yale University Press, 1994.

Johns Hopkins University, "Unrestricted Warfare Imperatives for Interagency Action: Integrating Strategy, Analysis & Technology." Unrestricted Warfare Symposium, March 2008. http://www.jhuapl.edu/urw_symposium/

Johnson, LTC David E. A. and Steve Pettit. " Principles of the Defense for Cyber Networks: An Executive Overview." *Defense Concepts*, Center for Advanced Defense Studies, Vol. 4, Ed. 4. December 2009. http://c4ads.org/sites/default/files/DefCon-January%202010.pdf

Johnston, Alastair I. *Cultural Realism: Strategic Culture and Grand Strategy in Chinese History.* Princeton, NJ: Princeton University Press, 1995.

Ka Po Ng. *Interpreting China's Military Power: Doctrine Makes Readiness.* New York, NY: Frank Cass, 2005.

Kraska,James and Brian Wilson, "China Wages Maritime Lawfare," *Foreign Policy*, 12 March, 2009. http://experts.foreignpolicy.com/posts/2009/03/11/china_wages_maritime_lawfare

Larry R. Jordan, Jr., MAJ USA. "Hybrid War: Is the U.S. Army Ready for the Face of 21st Century Warfare?" U.S. Army Command and General Staff College, Fort Leavenworth, KS. 2008.

Lee, Tsunghsi, Major, Taiwan Marine Corps. "Unrestricted Warfare: A Chinese Vision of Future War." Command and Staff College, Quantico, VA. 2003.

Libicki, Martin C. *Chinese Use of Cyberwar as an Anti-Access Strategy, Two Scenarios: RAND Corporation Testimony presented before the U.S. China Economic and Security Review Commission,* 27 January, 2011.

Lowrey, Annie. "Pentagon, bankers, prepare for financial warfare." *Foreign Policy*, 9 April 2009. http://blog.foreignpolicy.com/posts/2009/04/09/pentagon_bankers_prepare_for_financial_warfare

Mark Burles and Abram N. Shulsky. *Patterns in China's Use of Force: Evidence from History and Doctrinal Writings* (Santa Monica, CA: Rand, 2000), 79-93. Reader I, pp.161-176

Masur, Daniel R. "Adapting to Unrestricted Warfare." U.S. Army War College, Carlisle Barracks, PA. 22 March 2007.

McAfee Report. *Unsecured Economies: Protecting Vital Information.* Santa Clara, CA: McAfee, Inc., 2009.

Office of the President of the United States. *National Security Strategy of the United States of America.* Washington DC: The White House, May 2010.

Office of the President of the United States. *Cyberspace Policy Review, Assuring a Trusted and Resilient Information and Communications Infrastructure*, Washington DC. May 2011.

Office of the Secretary of Defense. *Annual Report to Congress: Military and Security Developments Involving the People's Republic of China.* Washington DC: Department of Defense, 2011.

Qiao Liang and Wang Xiangsui. *Unrestricted Warfare: China's Master Plan to Destroy America.* Panama City, Panama: Pan American Pub., 2002, 155-171.

Record, Jeffrey. *The American Way of War: Cultural Barriers to Successful Counterinsurgency.* Policy Analysis 577. Washington DC: CATO Institute, 2006.

Report on China's WTO Compliance, USTR, December 2009, www.ustr.gov/webfm_send/1572

Santoli, Albert. *Testimony before the U.S.-China Economic and Security Review Commission: China's Strategic Reach into Latin America.* 21 July 2005. http://www.uscc.gov/hearings/2005hearings/written_testimonies/05_07_21_22wrts/santoli_albert_wrts

Shambaugh, David. "Coping with a Conflicted China". *The Washington Quarterly*, 34:1 (Winter 2011): pp. 7-27.

Smith, Rupert. "The Utility of Force: The Art of War in the Modern World," New York: Knopf, 2005.

Trooboff, Peter D. *Law and Responsibility in Warfare.* Chapel Hill, NC: The Univ of North Carolina Press, 1975.

U.S.-China Economic and Security Review Commission. *Annual Report to Congress*, 2009. www.uscc.goc/index.php.

Van Messel, John A., Major USMC. "Unrestricted Warfare: A Chinese doctrine for future warfare?" Command and Staff College, Quantico, VA. 2005.

Vicente, Joao, Major, Portuguese Air Force. "Beyond the Box Thinking on Future War: The Art and Science of Unrestricted Warfare." Air Command and Staff College, Maxwell AFB, AL. April 2009.

Walton, Timoth. "Treble Spyglass, Treble Spear?: China's Three Warfares." *Defense Concepts*, Center for Advanced Defense Studies, Vol. 4, Ed. 4. December 2009. http://c4ads.org/sites/default/files/DefCon-January%202010.pdf

_______. *Capstone Concept for Joint Operations, Version 3.0.* Washington DC: Department of Defense, 15 January, 2009.

_______. *Joint Operating Concept, Irregular Warfare: Countering Irregular Threats, Version 2.0,* Washington DC: Department of Defense, 17 May, 2010

_______. *National Defense Strategy of the United States of America.* Washington DC: Department of Defense, June 2008.

_______. *National Military Strategy of the United States of America.* Washington DC: Department of Defense, 2011.

________. *China's National Defense in 2008.* Information Office of the State Council of the People's Republic of China, Beijing China, January 2009. http://english.gov.cn/official/2009-01/20/content_1210227.htm

_________. "China Begins Unrestricted Warfare." *News Max*, 25 Aug 2005. http://archive.newsmax.com/archives/articles/2005/8/25/121537.shtml,

Notes

[1] Clausewitz, "On War," 75, 149.

[2] Liang and Xiangsui, "Unrestricted Warfare," 2.

[3] Liang and Xiangsui, "Unrestricted Warfare," 56

[4] Vicente, "Beyond the Box, Thinking on Future War," The format for this table is a close duplicate of the one shown in Maj Vincente's 2009 Air Command and Staff College Research Paper. The information contained in the table is from Liang and Xiangsui's *Unrestricted Warfare* paper, 50-56, and 146.

[5] Liang and Xiangsui, *Unrestricted Warfare*, 7.

[6] Joint Pub 1-02, "Joint Terms and Definitions," 180.

[7] CENSA, "Hybrid Warfare and Transnational Threats," 1. This book, which was released in August 2011, contains 23 separate essays which provides examples of Hybrid wars, strategy development difficulties for Hybrid warfare, changes to military and government force structures, definitions, intelligence and interagency cooperation issues, a range of other ideas which focus on the Hybrid nature of future warfare.

[8] Hoffman, "The Hybrid Character of Modern Conflict," location 731, This quote was taken from Secretary Gate's article in Joint Force Quarterly (1st quarter, 2009) entitled "The National Defense Strategy: Striking the Right Balance."

[9] Hoffman, "The Hybrid Character of Modern Conflict," location 793.

[10] Clausewitz, "On War," 87.

[11] Jomini, "Summary of the Art of War," *The Art of War*, (Westport CT: Greenwood, 1971).

[12] Weigley, "The American Way of War: A History of United States Military Strategy and Policy,"

[13] Collin Gray, Irregular Enemies and the Essence of Strategy: Can the American Way of War Adapt? Chart of Grays 13 Characteristics is taken directly from Colin Gray's essay (See Appendix B for definitions of each characteristic)

1. Apolitical	8. Large-scale
2. Astrategic	9. Aggressive, offensive
3. Ahistorical	10. Profoundly regular
4. Problem-solving, optimistic	11. Impatient
5. Culturally challenged	12. Logistically excellent
6. Technology dependent	13. Highly sensitive to casualties
7. Focused on firepower	

[14] Keravuori, "Lost in Translation: The American Way of War," 2

[15] Keravuori, "Lost in Translation: The American Way of War," 1.

[16] Toner, Just War Criteria: A Brief Overview, AWC Dep of Leadership and Ethics

[17] Exploring Chinese History: Confucianism Core Concepts, http://ibiblio.org/chinesehistory

[18] Exploring Chinese History: Confucianism Core Concepts, http://ibiblio.org/chinesehistory

[19] Wikipedia, Sun Tzu, http://en.wikipedia.org/wiki/Sun_Tzu

[20] Ralph Sawyer, "The Art of War," Westview press, 1994, 13-14.

[21] Ralph Sawyer, Ralph, The Art of War,"

[22] Block I Reader, "The Art of War: Sun Zi's Military Methods," 149.

[23] Ebid

[24] Mark Burles and Abram Shulsky, "Patterns in China's Use of Force, " RAND Project Air Force, 2000, 89.

[25] Report to Congress, "Military Power of the People's Republic of China Fiscal Year 2007," 7.

[26] Report to Congress, "Military Power of the People's Republic of China Fiscal Year 2007," 7. The Chinese use the term "comprehensive strength" to gauge their security environment and determine how far along they are in the build-up compared to the rest of the world. Comprehensive strength (CP) is composed of two elements: comprehensive national power (CNP) and strategic configuration of power (SCP). CNP scores are based on "qualitative and quantitative measures of territory, natural resources, economic prosperity, diplomatic influence, international prestige, domestic cohesiveness, military capability, and cultural influence." SCP is roughly understood as an "alignment of forces." In their SCP estimate, Chinese strategic planners assess potential threats to their security and prosperity as well as opportunities that arise in the international community that might prompt adjustments to their national strategy.

[27] Peter Ford, "The Rise of an Economic Superpower: What does China Want" Christian Science Monitor, 2011.

[28] State Council of the People's Republic of China, China's National Defense in 2008," 7.

[29] Report to Congress, "Military Power of the People's Republic of China Fiscal Year 2011," 17.

[30] Information Office of the State Council of the People's Republic of China, China's National Defense 2008, 17.

[31] Report to Congress, "Military Power of the People's Republic of China Fiscal Year 2011," 25. The actual quote is as follows: "Striking only after the enemy has struck does not mean waiting for the enemy's strike passively... It doesn't mean to give up the "advantageous chances" in campaign or tactical operations, for the "first shot" on the plane of politics must be differentiated from the "first shot" on that of tactics...if any country or organization violates the other country's sovereignty and territorial integrity, the other side will have the right to "fire the first shot" on the plane of tactics."

[32] Report to Congress, "Military Power of the People's Republic of China Fiscal Year 2011," 13.

[33] Report to Congress, "U.S.-CHINA ECONOMIC AND SECURITY REVIEW COMMISSION, 2011, pg 201.

[34] Dunlap, "Lawfare: A Decisive Element of 21st Century Conflicts," Joint Force Quarterly, 3rd Qtr, 2009. pg 35

[35] Report to Congress, "Military Power of the People's Republic of China Fiscal Year 2011," 13.

[36] Tony Corn, "From War Managers to Soldier Diplomats: The Coming Revolution in Civil Military Relations, 2009 Small Wars Journal. David Kennedy, "Law Has Become a Military Instrument," Times Online, October 25, 2006, available at (www.timesonline.co.uk/tol/comment/article613078.ece).

[37] Report to Congress, "Military Power of the People's Republic of China Fiscal Year 2011," 25.

[38] Report to Congress, "Military Power of the People's Republic of China Fiscal Year 2007," 13.

[39] Charles Dulap, "Lawfare: A Decisive Element of 21st Century Conflict," Joint Force Quarterly, 3rd Qtr 2009, 39.

[40] Encyclopedia Britannica, http://www.britannica.com/EBchecked/topic/178545/economic-warfare

[41] CRS Report: Comparing Global Influence; pg 8

[42] Evan Ellis, "SSI: China-Latin America Engagement: Good Will, Good Business, And Strategic Position,"1.

[43] CRS Report: Comparing Global Influence; pg 11

[44] CRS Report: China-US Relations: Current Issues and Implications for US Policy; 9.

[45] Tyler Durden, China And Iran To Bypass Dollar, Plan Oil Barter System, And A Deeper Dive Into The Iranian Oil Bourse, http://www.zerohedge.com/news/china-and-iran-bypass-dollar-plan-oil-barter-system-and-deeper-dive-iranian-oil-bourse

[46] Elison Elliott, "Economic Warfare: China Threatens U.S. Debt as WMD," 2.

[47] Liang and Xiangsui, *Unrestricted Warfare*, 50.

[48] Daniel Ventre, "Chinese Information and Cyber Warfare," 3.

[49] Reuters, "State Actor behind slew of Cyber Attacks."

[50] Bennet, "2009 Report on the Capability of the People's Republic of China to Conduct Cyber Warfare and Computer Network Exploitation," 8.

[51] Siobhan Gorman & Julian Barnes, Pentagon Considers Cyber Attacks an Act of War, Wall Street Journal, May 11

[52] National Security Strategy, 34.

[53] 2011 US-China Economic and Security Review Commission Report to Congress, 1.

[54] Donna Miles, " Doctrine to Establish Rules of Engagement Against Cyber Attacks, American Forces Press Service, Oct. 20, 2011

[55] 2009 URW Symposium Notes_pg 12

[56] Christine E. Wormuth, "Is Gold Waters-Nichols needed for Homeland Security," 84.

[57] Beyond Goldwater-Nichols: U.S. Government and Defense Reform for a New Strategic Era: Functionally, the report is divided into two parts. Chapters 2-5 address ways to improve national security policymaking and execution on an interagency basis, while chapters 6-12 focus on the Department of Defense. The interagency recommendations share a broad theme: they aim to get the many disparate parts of the U.S. national security structure to work together, in both planning and execution.

[58] CRS Report: Comparing Global Influence; 15.

Annex A

Forms of Unrestricted Warfare*

1. **Financial Warfare:** entering and subverting banking and stock markets and manipulating the value of a targeted currency.
2. **Trade Warfare:** using trade measures for waging non-military warfare.
3. **Resource Warfare:** gaining control of scarce natural resources and being able to control or manipulate their access and market value.
4. **Economic Aid Warfare:** controlling a targeted country through aid dependency.
5. **Sanctions Warfare**: economic penalties, such as stoppage of trade and financial transactions, imposed upon a country to force compliance with another country's or the international community's demands.
6. **Regulations /Legal warfare:** joining international or multinational organizations in order to subvert their policies and the interpretation of legal rulings. Uses international and domestic law to claim the legal high ground or assert Chinese interests.
7. **Ecological /Environmental Warfare:** weakening or subjugating a rival nation by despoiling or altering its natural environment. Employing modern technology to adversely influence the natural state of rivers, oceans, the crust of the earth, the polar ice sheets, the air circulating in the atmosphere, and the ozone layer.
8. **Ideological Warfare**: The struggle to supplant or impose a rival form of government, religion, or racial concept. It is the declared belief of the warring nation that its way of life deserves to be imposed, or that its inspired interests must be served.
9. **Media Warfare:** manipulating foreign media, either by compromising or intimidating journalists or getting access to another country's airwaves and imposing your own national perspectives. Influence domestic and international public opinion to build support of one's actions and dissuade an adversary from pursing actions contrary to one's own interests.
10. **Cultural Warfare:** influencing the cultural biases of a targeted country by imposing your own cultural viewpoints

11. **Diplomatic Warfare:** use of diplomacy to influence international bodies (such as the UN), other nations, and domestic audiences to support a course of action against another nation. The passage of a UN resolution that authorizes sanctions or the use of force would be an example of successfully diplomatic warfare.

12. **Network warfare:** dominating or subverting transnational information systems.

13. **Intelligence Warfare:** the use of various intelligence collection assets or methods to gain a clear understanding of a potential adversary's strengths, weaknesses, capabilities, or intent and to deny this information about yourself.

14. **Psychological warfare:** imposing one's national interest by dominating a rival nation's perception of its own strengths and weaknesses. Operations designed to deterring, shocking, and demoralizing enemy military personnel and supporting civilian populations.

15. **Smuggling Warfare:** sabotaging a rival country's economy by flooding its markets with illegal goods; jeopardizing a local economy by flooding the market with pirated products.

16. **Drug Warfare:** flooding illicit drugs across national borders and breaking down the fabric of a society through their use.

17. **Fabrication Warfare:** presenting a counterfeit appearance of real strength before the eyes of the enemy.

18. **Technological Warfare:** gaining control or having edge in particular vital technologies that can be used in both peace and wartime.

19. **Tactical Warfare:** utilizing conventional and unconventional means to influence battles and individual engagements.

20. **Atomic Warfare:** the use of nuclear weapons to achieve your aims

21. **Conventional Warfare:** the use of conventional military forces to achieve aims

22. **Bio-Chemical Warfare:** the use of biological weapons to achieve your aims

23. **Space Warfare**: Military confrontations mainly conducted in outer space between two rival parties. It includes military offensive and defensive operations in outer space, operations conducted to engage targets in air space or on the ground from outer space, as well as operations conducted from the ground or in air space aimed at destroying or incapacitating space systems.

24. **Guerrilla Warfare:** a form of irregular warfare; conflicts in which a small group of combatants including, but not limited to, armed civilians (or "irregulars") use military tactics, such as ambushes, sabotage, raids, the element of surprise, and extraordinary mobility to harass a larger and less-mobile traditional army, or strike a vulnerable target, and withdraw almost immediately.

25. **Terror Warfare**: Two forms, traditional and "new" terror war. Traditional is not bound by any of the traditional rules of society. It is characterized by the use of limited resources to fight an unlimited war. These resources have traditionally been bombings, kidnappings, assassinations, and plane hijackings. The "new" terror war is the use of new technologies and "super-weapons" to cause massive casualties against an enemy population or military force.

*Note: Several of the forms of URW identified by Colonel's Liang and Xiangsui are not defined in their concept paper. Therefore, the definitions in this Annex are from multiple sources, to include Col Liang and Xiangsui URW concept paper, pgs 50-56, 146, Major John Van Messel's paper "Unrestricted Warfare: A Chinese Doctrine for Future Warfare?," and online dictionaries.

Annex B

Collin Gray's Characteristics of the American Way of War*

1. **Apolitical**: "Americans are wont to regard war and peace as sharply distinctive conditions. The U.S. military has a long history of waging war for the goal of victory, paying scant regard to the consequences of the course of its operations for the character of the peace that will follow."

2. **Astrategic**: "Strategy is, or should be, the bridge that connects military power with policy. When Americans wage war as a largely autonomous activity, leaving worry about peace and its politics to some later day, the strategy bridge has broken down."

3. **Ahistorical**: "America is a future-oriented, still somewhat 'new' country, one that has a founding ideology of faith in, and hope for, and commitment to, human betterment. It is only to be expected, therefore, that Americans should be less than highly respectful of what they might otherwise allow history to teach them."

4. **Problem-Solving, Optimistic**: "The American way in war is not easily discouraged or deflected once it is exercised with serious intent to succeed. . . . The problem-solving faith, the penchant for the 'engineering fix,' has the inevitable consequence of leading U.S. policy, including its use of armed force, to attempt the impossible."

5. **Culturally Ignorant**: Americans are not inclined "to be respectful of the beliefs, habits, and behaviors of other cultures . . .the American way of war has suffered from the self-inflicted damage caused by a failure to understand the enemy of the day."

6. **Technologically Dependent**: "America is the land of technological marvels and of extraordinary technology dependency. . . . American soldiers say that the human beings matter most, but in practice the American way of war, past, present, and prospectively future, is quintessentially and uniquely technologically dependent."

7. **Firepower Focused:** "It has long been the American way in warfare to send metal in harm's way in place of vulnerable flesh. . . .Needless to say, perhaps, a devotion to firepower, while highly desirable in itself, cannot help but encourage the U.S. armed forces to rely on it even when other modes of military behavior would be more suitable. In irregular conflicts in particular . . . resorting to firepower solutions readily becomes self-defeating."

8. **Large-Scale:** "Poor societies are obliged to wage war frugally. They have no choice other than to attempt to fight smarter than rich enemies. The United States has been blessed with wealth in all its forms. Inevitably, the U.S. armed forces, once mobilized and equipped, have fought a rich person's war. They could hardly do otherwise."

9. **Aggressive and Offensive**. Geopolitics, culture, and material endowment have combined to pull the American way of war towards an aggressive offensive style. Because of America's geopolitical isolation, a product of geography and culture, in the 20th century the country repeatedly joined in wars that already were well underway. America had to take the initiative and move men and material across oceans. Also, it was obliged to commit to offensive operations in order to take back the gains made by enemies in Europe and Asia at the outset of their rampages of conquest....Americans sought to take war to the enemy, as rapidly and destructively as the machines of industrial age warfare permitted.

10. **Profoundly Regular**: "Few, if any, armies have been equally competent in the conduct of regular and irregular warfare. . . .As institutions, however, the U.S. armed forces have not been friendly either to irregular warfare or to those in its ranks who were would-be practitioners and advocates of what was regarded as the sideshow of insurgency. American soldiers . . . have always been prepared nearly exclusively for 'real war,' which is to say combat against a tolerably symmetrical, regular enemy."

11. **Impatient**: "Americans have approached warfare as a regrettable occasional evil that has to be concluded as decisively and rapidly as possible."

12. **Logistically Excellent**: "Americans at war have been exceptionally able logisticians. With a continental-size interior and an effectively insular geographic location, such ability has been mandatory if the country was to wage war at all, let alone wage it effectively. . . . A large logistical footprint . . . requires a great deal of guarding, helps isolate American troops from local people and their culture, and generally tends to grow."

13. **Sensitivity to Casualties:** "In common with the Roman Empire, the American guardian of world order is much averse to suffering a high rate of military casualties. . . Both superstates had and have armies that are small, too small in the opinion of many, relative to their responsibilities Moreover, well-trained professional soldiers, volunteers all, are expensive to raise, train, and retain, and are difficult to replace." American society, it is said, "has become so sensitive to casualties that the domestic context for U.S. military action is no longer tolerant of bloody adventures in muscular imperial governance."

*Note: The definitions above are taken directly from Jeffrey Record's 2006 essay, "The American Way of War, Cultural Barriers to Successful Counterinsurgency." Due to the length of Collin Grey's description of his 13 characteristics, Jeffrey Record's excellent summaries of Collin Grey's characteristics are provided in this annex as a quick reference to their meaning. For the complete description of the characteristics, refer to Collin Grey's 2006 essay, "Irregular Enemies and the Essence of Strategy: Can the American Way of War Adapt?" pages 30-49.

Annex C*

Timeline of Significant Chinese Related Cyber Events (1999-2010)

1. 1999, May: Accidental bombing of China's Belgrade embassy provokes defacement of numerous US government sites.
2. 1999, August: "Taiwanese-Chinese Hacker War" erupts.
3. 2000, May: Chinese Hackers deface sites across Taiwan.
4. 2000, October: Chinese Hackers again threaten DDOS and Web Defacements on Taiwan's National Day.
5. 2001, April: first "Sino-US Hacker War" erupts after US EP-3 and PLA F-8 Collide and US crew is detained.
6. 2002, May: Hacker activity marking the Anniversary of the first Sino-US Hacker war is squashed by the Chinese government; Chinese hacktivism appears to go underground.
7. 2003, August: Reports of Chinese hackers against Taiwanese government and commercial sites.
8. 2004, July: Chinese hackers attack against Taiwan continue.
9. 2004, November: Media reports of attacks against several US military installations.
10. 2005, March: Several attacks from sites allegedly in China against multiple sites in Japan.
11. 2005, August: Media reporting of Chinese cyber espionage ring codenamed "Titian Rain."
12. 2005, September: According to media staff of the Taiwan National Security Council is targeted via socially registered email.
13. 2006, June: Chinese hackers strike Taiwan's MoD.
14. 2006, July: Media reports US State Department is recovering from a damaging cyber attack.
15. 2006, August: Official state hostile Chinese cyber forces have downloaded up to 20TB of data.
16. 2006, August: Claim of a Congressional computer being hacked are made.
17. 2006, November: US Naval War College computer infrastructure reportedly attacked.
18. 2007, June: OSD computers attacked via malicious email.
19. 2007, August: Reports emerge on cyber attacks Germany.
20. 2007, September: Reports emerge on cyber attacks against UK.
21. 2007, September: Reports emerge on cyber attacks against New Zealand.
22. 2007, October: US Nuclear Labs targeted by malicious email.
23. 2007, December: MI-5 issues warning on Chinese Cyber attacks.
24. 2008, March: Reports emerge on cyber attacks against Australia.
25. 2008, April: Reports emerge on cyber attacks against India.
26. 2008, May: Reports emerge on cyber attacks against Belgium
27. 2008, June: US elections campaign hacking reported.
28. 2008, November: Hacking of White House Computer alleged.
29. 2008, November: Reports of a massive, sustained intrusion into NASA systems released.
30. 2008, December: French Embassy Web site attacked in protest over meeting with Dalai Lama.

31. 2009, April: Compromise of systems across 103 countries by Chinese cyber spies while Chinese Government denies involvement in GhostNet.
32. 2009, April: Daily attacks reported against German Government.
33. 2009, April: Chinese government denies reports of hacking the Australian Prime Minister's email.
34. 2009, April: Reports emerge of Chinese hackers targeting South Korea officials with socially engineered email.
35. 2009, April: Lockheed Martin and the F-35 Joint Strike Fighter program files compromised by hackers.
36. 2009, December: Operation Aurora was a cyber-attack which began in mid-2009 and continued through December 2009 which targeted Google as well as several other internet and defense industry corporations.
37. 2010, January: Report released that several US oil companies systems were compromised by hackers in 2008 and 2009.
38. 2010, August: The Pentagon released statement warning that The People's Liberation Army is using "information warfare units'' to develop viruses to attack computer systems and networks, and those units include civilian computer professionals.
39. 2010, October: Australian Military reports a 203% increase in cyber-attacks in 2010.
40. 2010, December: US government reports a 39% increase in cyber-attacks in 2010.

* Almost all the information for this annex is taken directly from the 2009 US-China Economic and Security Review Commission Report on the Capability of the People's Republic of China to Conduct Cyber Warfare and Computer Network Exploitation." Page 67.